T0113541

THE SECRET

— OF —

LIFE

A COMPOSITION
OF QUOTES

DAVID F. COMBS

authorHOUSE®

AuthorHouse™
1663 Liberty Drive
Bloomington, IN 47403
www.authorhouse.com
Phone: 833-262-8899

Published by AuthorHouse 09/23/2020

ISBN: 978-1-7283-7218-1 (sc)
ISBN: 978-1-7283-7221-1 (e)

Library of Congress Control Number: 2020916513

Print information available on the last page.

"The secret of life is enjoying the passage of time" … "It's a lovely ride"

James Taylor

"There is only one happiness in life, to love and to be loved."

George Sand

"This above all: to thine own self be true."

William Shakespeare

FOREWORD

Although not a very original title, *The Secret of Life* is intended to be an inspirational collection of quotes, sayings, song lyrics and book excerpts from various authors, lyricists and famous/historical figures … compiled by this amateur author (with some personal thoughts/comments thrown in) … to hopefully help people through various stages of life's "journey".

Inspired by (and frequently quoted/referenced in this book) Michael A. Singer's ***The Untethered Soul: the journey beyond yourself*** *(New Harbinger Publications/Noetic Books; 1 edition, 2007, with permission conveyed through Copyright Clearance Center, Inc.)*, and through my own personal search for Self-awareness and understanding of the mysteries of life/death, this compilation should have broad appeal for anyone who has gone through, or is going through: Fear, Hopelessness, Grief, Heartache, Self-Discovery, Anticipation, Joy, Happiness, Self-Doubt, Worry, Pain, Religious Conflict, Love, Loss, Spiritual Enlightenment, and more of life's endless challenges.

Dedicated to
Nancy Elizabeth Bohart (Combs)

CONTENTS

INTRODUCTION

In an attempt to better understand *The Untethered Soul* (after reading it for the third time), I looked to other references and quotes that complement Mr. Singer's inspirational and thought-provoking teachings about Self-Awareness, Consciousness, and inner Spirituality. You will notice that many of the supporting quotes & excerpts are not from philosophers, theologians or 'great thinkers' (intentionally). In searching through thousands of quotes and excerpts on myriad subjects, I chose those that had some tie-in with topics and key words in *The Untethered Soul* (regardless of the 'author's credentials'.)

THE BIG PICTURE

Life, the Universe and Everything
-   **Douglas Adams**

That about sums it up ... *and the answer is not 42.*

"Life is just something we watch unfold."
-   **Forest** (*DEVS*)

To me, this may be the simple overarching message from Mr. Singer ... actually *doing* it is the challenge, i.e. the constant journey. We should 'witness' our inner voice, our heart, our pain as we would any external object ... while we remain separate from (i.e. behind) the incessant chatter, worry, fear and pointless problem-solving that goes on inside our head constantly.

"In case you haven't noticed, you have a mental dialogue going on inside your head that never stops. It just keeps going and going. Have you ever wondered why it talks in there? How does it decide what to say and when to say it? ... How much of what it says is even important? And if right now you are hearing, 'I don't know what you're talking about. I don't have any voice inside my head!' – that's the voice we're talking about."

"There is nothing more important to true growth than realizing that you are not the voice of the mind - you are the one who hears it"

- **Singer, Michael A**. *The Untethered Soul: the journey beyond yourself*, New Harbinger / Noetic Books, 2007

My interpretation – to attain true inner freedom and happiness, one must learn to *objectively* observe (Witness) your problems instead of being lost in them. Again, easier said than done.

"Ramana Maharashi (1879-1950), a great teacher in the yogic tradition, used to say that to attain inner freedom one must continuously and sincerely ask the question, 'Who am I?' He taught that this was more important than reading books, learning mantras, or going to holy places. Just ask, 'Who am I? Who sees when I see? Who hears when I hear? Who knows that I am aware? Who am I?"

"There is nothing higher or deeper than consciousness. Consciousness is pure awareness."

"If you go very deep, that is where you live. You live in the seat of consciousness. A true spiritual being lives there, without effort and without intent. Just as you effortlessly look outside and see all that you see, you will eventually sit far enough back inside to see all your thoughts and emotions, as well as the outer form. ... Now you are in your center of consciousness. You are behind everything, just watching. ... That center is the seat of the Buddhist

Self, the Hindu Atman, and the Judeo-Christian Soul. The great mystery begins once you take that seat deep within."

- **Singer, Michael A**. *The Untethered Soul: the journey beyond yourself,* New Harbinger / Noetic Books, 2007

"This is the secret of life: The Self lives only by dying, finds its identity (and its happiness) only by self-forgetfulness, self-giving, self-sacrifice, and agape love."

- **Peter Kreeft** (*Jesus-Shock*)

"He who is not every day conquering some fear has not learned the secret of life."

- **Shannon L. Adler**

"No matter how many plans you make or how much in control you are, life is always winging it."

- **Carroll Bryant**

"The secret of life is meaningless unless you find it yourself."

- **W. Somerset Maugham** (*Of Human Bondage*)

"All goes onward and outward, nothing collapses, And to die is different from what anyone supposed, and luckier."

- **Walt Whitman**

"Only when you accept that one day you'll die can you let go, and make the best out of life. And that's the big secret. That's the miracle."

- **abriel Bá** (*Daytripper*)

"Krishna was once asked what was the most miraculous thing in all creation, and he replied, 'That a man should wake each morning and believe deep in his heart that he will live forever, even though he knows that he is doomed.'
-   **Christopher Pike** (*Phantom, The Last Vampire, #4*)

"There is no cure for birth and death save to enjoy the interval."
-   **George Santayana**

"Humans are the only race who are continuously either possessed by or obsessed for various energies."
-   **Ramana Pemmaraju**

"It will encourage you to take the plunge into the unknown and mystery of your own life where every action becomes an effortless, appropriate response to whatever life brings you."
-   **Mark J. Johnson** (*Life as Play*)

"The great beauty of life is its mystery, the inability to know what course our life will take, and diligently work to transmute into our final form based upon a lifetime of constant discovery and enterprising effort. Accepting the unknown and unknowable eliminates regret."
-   **Kilroy J. Oldster** (*Dead Toad Scrolls*)

"I truly don't know what will happen in my life, and I don't want to know. My life will unfold the way it needs to. Having to know kept me caught in my head. Not needing to know keeps me open to the great mystery of life."
-   **Mary O'Malley**

"So, there are two ways you can live: you can devote your life to staying in your comfort zone, or you can work on your freedom. In other words, you can devote your whole life to the process of making sure everything fits within your limited model, or you can devote your life to freeing yourself from the limits of your model."

"Would you like to go beyond? … Imagine a comfort zone that is so expanded that it can easily fill the entire day, no matter what happens. The day unfolds and the mind doesn't say anything. You simply interact with the day with a peaceful, fully inspired heart. … You realize that you will always be fine. Nothing can ever bother you. … Then one day, when you least expect it, you fall through to the infinite. That is what it means to go beyond."

- **Singer, Michael A**. *The Untethered Soul: the journey beyond yourself*, New Harbinger / Noetic Books, 2007

And now for the 'lighter side' of the Big Picture …

"Don't Panic!"

"On planet Earth, man had always assumed that he was more intelligent than dolphins because he had achieved so much – the wheel, New York, wars and so on – whilst all the dolphins had ever done was muck about in the water having a good time. But conversely, the dolphins had always believed that they were more intelligent than man – for precisely the same reasons."

(the dolphins' final message to man), "So long, and thanks for all the fish!"

"If there's anything more important than Ego around, I want it caught and shot now."
"Time is an illusion – Lunchtime doubly so."
"I'd rather be happy than right any day."

"Space is big. You just won't believe how vastly, hugely, mind-bogglingly big it is. I mean you may think it's a long way down the road to the chemist's, but that's just peanuts to space."

- **Douglas Adams** (*The Hitchhiker's Guide to the Galaxy, #1*) (*Life, the Universe and Everything*)

"Walk outside on a clear night and just look up into the sky. You are sitting on a planet spinning around in the middle of absolutely nowhere. Though you can only see a few thousand stars, there are hundreds of billions of stars in our Milky Way Galaxy alone. In fact, it is estimated that there are over a trillion stars in the Spiral Galaxy. And that galaxy would look like one star to us, if we could even see it. You're just standing on one little ball of dirt and spinning around one of the stars. ... You came here to visit for a handful of years and then you're going to leave. ... If you have to be here, at least be happy and enjoy the experience."

- **Singer, Michael A**. *The Untethered Soul: the journey beyond yourself,* New Harbinger / Noetic Books, 2007

Too big? Too hard to contemplate? It is for me, although I have been trying each night to do just this. Personally, I can have the same "ego-humbling" experience by just looking out on the ocean or even just observing the other miracles of nature, e.g. a tree or flower, a river, a soaring hawk, or a majestic mountain. Even on this microcosmic scale, our individual insignificance can seem profound.

"Everybody thinks of changing humanity, but nobody thinks of changing himself."
- **Leo Tolstoy**

"Flow with whatever is happening and let your mind be free. Stay centered by accepting whatever you are doing. This is the ultimate."
- **Chuang Tzu**

"The difference between great people and everyone else is that great people create their lives actively, while everyone else is created by their lives, passively waiting to see where life takes them next. The difference between the two is the difference between living fully and just existing."
- **Michael E. Gerber**

"My will shall shape my future. Whether I fail or succeed shall be no man's doing but my own. I am the force; I can clear any obstacle before me or I can be lost in the maze. My choice; my responsibility; win or lose, only I hold the key to my destiny."
- **Elaine Maxwell**

"Today you are You, that is truer than true. There is no one alive who is Youer than You."
- **Dr. Seuss**

LOVE / THE HEART

"The secret of love is in opening up your heart. It's okay to feel afraid, but don't let that stand in your way. Cause anyone knows that love is the only road."
- **James Taylor**

"The spiritual concept of love is not a feeling or emotion. It is a state of awareness."
- **Anthon St. Maarten**

"When someone loves you for who you are (completely) without judgment, impossible conditions or pretense... your heart awakens, your soul comes alive, your senses are stimulated and you know true happiness."
- **Carlos Wallace** (*The Other 99 T.Y.M.E.S: Train Your Mind to Enjoy Serenity*)

"The beginning of love is to let those we love be perfectly themselves, and not to twist them to fit our own image. Otherwise we love only the reflection of ourselves we find in them."
- **Thomas Merton**

"Love has nothing to do with what you are expecting to get - only with what you are expecting to give - which is everything."
- **Katherine Hepburn**

"Since love grows within you, so beauty grows. For love is the beauty of the soul."
-   **Saint Augustine**

"All, everything that I understand, I understand only because I love."
-   **Leo Tolstoy**

"I asked myself, 'What do I want more than happiness?' and there was only one answer - the only thing that trumps happiness is love. Not the kind of love we are normally taught about, but the kind of unconditional love that is a deep inner state which doesn't depend on any person, situation or a romantic partner. That's how I define Love for No Reason: it's an inner state of love."
-   **Marci Schimoff**

"What it's like to be a parent: It's one of the hardest things you'll ever do but in exchange it teaches you the meaning of unconditional love."
-   **Nicholas Sparks**

"LIFE = UNCONDITIONAL LOVE
If you can feel this equation. I said IF you can FEEL this equation you can solve any mystery in life."
-   **Sargot Singh**

"Love the animals, love the plants, love everything. If you love everything, you will perceive the divine mystery in things. Once you perceive it, you will begin to comprehend

it better every day. And you will come at last to love the whole world with an all-embracing love."
- **Fyodor Dostoevsky**

"This fire that we call Loving is too strong for human minds. But just right for human souls."
- **Aberjhani**

"The world cannot be discovered by a journey of miles...only by a spiritual journey...by which we arrive at the ground at our feet, and learn to be at home. The ultimate lesson all of us have to learn is unconditional love, which includes not only others but ourselves as well."
- **Elizabeth Kubler-Ross**

"Unconditional love really exists in each of us. It is part of our deep inner being. It is not so much an active emotion as a state of being."
- **Ram Dass**

"Learn to pay attention to your body with the relaxed attitude of gratitude, trust, curiosity and unconditional love rather than being pushed around by habit, fear, anxiety, social customs, other people's schedules and other people's ideas about what is good for you."
- **Wallace D. Wattles**

"When you can completely love your ego unconditionally and accept it as part of how you express in this life, you'll no longer have a problem with it. It won't impede your growth - on the contrary, it will be an asset."
- **Anita Moorjani**

"The people who help us grow toward true self offer unconditional love, neither judging us to be deficient nor trying to force us to change but accepting us exactly as we are. And yet this unconditional love does not lead us to rest on our laurels. Instead, it surrounds us with a charged force field that makes us want to grow from the inside out - a force field that is safe enough to take the risks and endure the failures that growth requires."
- **Parker J. Palmer**

"Love feels no burden, thinks nothing of trouble, attempts what is above its strength, pleads no excuse of impossibility; for it thinks all things lawful for itself, and all things possible."
- **Thomas a Kempis**

"Happiness does not depend on what you have or who you are. It solely relies on what you think."
- **Buddha**

"Happiness cannot be traveled to, owned, earned, worn, or consumed. Happiness is the spiritual experience of living every minute with love, grace, and gratitude."
- **Denis Waitley**

"The most important thing is to enjoy your life—to be happy—it's all that matters."
- **Audrey Hepburn**

"Beauty is not in the face; beauty is a light in the heart."
- **Kahil Gibran**

"Every mystery of life has its origin in the heart."
- **Hans Urs von Balthasar** (*Heart of the World*)

"The only lasting beauty is the beauty of the heart"
- **Rumi**

"The best and most beautiful things in the world cannot be seen or even touched - they must be felt with the heart."
- **Helen Keller**

"All the knowledge I possess everyone else can acquire, but my heart is all my own."
- **Johann Wolfgang von Goethe**

"Nobody has ever measured, not even poets, how much the heart can hold."
- **Zelda Fitzgerald**

"You change your life by changing your heart."
- **Max Lucado**

"Have patience with everything that remains unsolved in your heart. ... live in the question."
- **Rainer Maria Rilke** (*Letters to a Young Poet*)

"The heart ... is an energy center, a chakra. It is one of the most beautiful and powerful energy centers, and one that affects our daily lives. ... You feel your heart's energy all the time. Think about what it is like to feel love in your heart ... to feel inspiration and enthusiasm pour from your heart ... to feel energy well up in your heart making you confident and strong. All of this happens because the heart is an energy center."

- **Singer, Michael A**. *The Untethered Soul: the journey beyond yourself,* New Harbinger / Noetic Books, 2007

Personally, this whole concept of inner energy fascinates me, as it is a topic Nancy and I discussed many times before her passing in 2017, and one that I have thought about a lot more since her death. We all learned about the first law of thermodynamics, also known as the **Law of Conservation of Energy**, which states that energy can neither be created nor destroyed; energy can only be transferred or changed from one form to another. So, if our inner energy (our soul, if you will) is actual 'energy', and it can't be destroyed, it must transmute into another form of energy at the time of our death, right? Of course, no one knows what this 'next step' entails, but all religions address the Big Question of life after death in one way or another. *Arguably, it might be the primary benefit/purpose of religion.*

Nancy envisioned her energy dissipating into the universe, perhaps becoming part of a star/sun. I, on the other hand, probably because of my larger ego, believe that our inner energy (i.e. soul) remains in tact and simply moves on to the next plain (whatever that is) after we are "untethered" from this world. But the fact is, it doesn't really matter what we believe – and it is certainly a waste of 'energy' to worry about it – because there is one truth we all know about death – it will happen. So, the Biq Question really should be about Life *before* Death, and how we choose to open our hearts and experience "the journey beyond yourself" *during* our lifetime.

"The fear of death follows from the fear of life. A man who lives fully is prepared to die at any time."
- **Mark Twain**

"To live is the rarest thing in the world. Most people exist, that is all."
- **Oscar Wilde**

"In the end, enjoying life's experiences is the only rational thing to do. ... You're going to die anyway. Things are going to happen anyway. Why shouldn't you be happy? You gain nothing by being bothered by life's events. It doesn't change the world; you just suffer."

"Do not let anything that happens in life be important enough that you're willing to close your heart over it."
- **Singer, Michael A**. *The Untethered Soul: the journey beyond yourself,* New Harbinger / Noetic Books, 2007

SELF-REFLECTION & INTROSPECTION

We have been taught that we, as humans, only use a small percentage of our brain's capacity. Is it just a matter of evolution, OR is there a way to tap into this resource during our lifetime? I wonder what we could contemplate and achieve if we had access to that large 'unused' capacity? Is this where genius lies, where musical prodigy or autism comes from, where astral projection happens, where miracles occur, or where 'enlightenment' dwells?

(from Encyclopedia Britannica) **Introspection**, (from Latin *introspicere*, "to look within"), the process of observing the operations of one's own mind with a view to discovering the laws that govern the mind. In a dualistic philosophy, which divides the natural world (matter, including the human body) from the contents of consciousness, introspection is the chief method of psychology.

"Introspection encourages positive energy from oneself to enhance personal motivation to learn more about themselves. It makes it easier to break down things that distract us or lead to negative thoughts by establishing a process of analyzing and purifying thoughts and feelings."

"The Greek philosopher Plato has influenced developments of introspection, along with the aspect of human self-reflection. His beliefs included not just reviewing one's thoughts, but to be thorough in examining how they appear within us. Introspection is exercised by the human ability to be willing to learn more about one's nature and purpose. Philosophy of the mind, self-awareness, and consciousness also play essential roles in self-reflection."

- **Tanisha Herrin** (*What Is Introspection?: Psychology, Definition, And Applications*)

"… when you look deep within your soul, introspection creeps in. By employing your internal energies, you can certainly attain peace. How do you connect with that energy?

It is through your mind. Because when you ponder, you tend to tap more into that inner self. As a result, you tend to question your purpose of existence on this planet. Hence the stronger the mind's energy the more at peace (soulful) you'd feel."

- **Valerie Soleil** (*4 Ways Introspection Helps You Reconnect with Your True Self*)

"Never regret the things that make you smile. Introspection is the element to spiritual growth."

- **Malika E Nura**

"Many people suffer from the fear of finding oneself alone, and so they don't find themselves at all."

- **Rollo May** (*Man's Search for Himself*)

"The only journey is the one within."

- **Rainer Maria Rilke**

"Vision is a beautiful picture clicked with the roll of soul involving mind and heart to do introspection of the past, reflection of the present and connection with the future to see things considered impossible as possible."

- **Anuj Somany**

"My friend...care for your psyche...know thyself, for once we know ourselves, we may learn how to care for ourselves"

- **Socrates**

"To find out what is truly individual in ourselves, profound reflection is needed; and suddenly we realize how uncommonly difficult the discovery of individuality is."

- **C.G. Jung**

"If the whole universe can be found in our own body and mind, this is where we need to make our inquires. We all have the answers within ourselves, we just have not got in touch with them yet. The potential of finding the truth within requires faith in ourselves."

- **Ayya Khema**

"Stop looking to the sky for answers. The light isn't above you. It's within you."

- **Elysia Lumen Strife** (*Shadows of the Son*)

FEAR & PAIN

"Fear is the cause of every problem. It's the root of all prejudices and the negative emotions of anger, jealousy, and possessiveness. If you had no fear, you could be perfectly happy living in this world."

"The psyche is built upon avoiding ... pain, and as a result, it has fear of pain as its foundation. That is what caused the psyche to be. To understand this, notice that if the feeling of rejection is a major problem for you, you will fear experiences that cause rejection. That fear will become part of your psyche. Even though the actual events causing rejection are infrequent, you will have to deal with the fear of rejection all the time. That is how we create a pain that is always there. If you are doing something to avoid pain, then pain is running your life. All of your thoughts and feelings will be affected by your fears."

"Wise beings do not want to remain a slave to the fear of pain. They permit the world to be what it is instead of being afraid of it. They wholeheartedly participate in life, but not for the purpose of using life to avoid themselves. If life does something that causes a disturbance inside of you, instead of pulling away, let it pass through you like the wind. After all, things happen every day that cause inner disturbance. At any moment you can feel frustration, anger, fear, jealousy, insecurity, or embarrassment. If you watch, you will see that the heart is trying to push it all away. If you want to be free, you have to learn to stop fighting these human feelings."

- **Singer, Michael A**. *The Untethered Soul: the journey beyond yourself,* New Harbinger / Noetic Books, 2007

"I must say a word about fear. It is life's only true opponent. Only fear can defeat life. It is a clever, treacherous adversary, how well I know. It has no decency, respects no law or convention, shows no mercy. It goes for your weakest spot, which it finds with unnerving ease. It begins in your mind, always ... so you must fight hard to express it. You must fight hard to shine the light of words upon it. Because if you don't, if your fear becomes a wordless darkness that you avoid, perhaps even manage to forget, you open yourself to further attacks of fear because you never truly fought the opponent who defeated you."

- **Yann Martel** (*Life of Pi*)

"People fear death even more than they fear pain. It's strange that they fear death. Life hurts more than death. At the point of death, the pain is over."

- **Jim Morrison**

"It is not death that a man should fear, but he should fear never beginning to live."

- **Marcus Aurelius** (*Meditations*)

"I'm not afraid of death; I just don't want to be there when it happens."

- **Woody Allen**

"There is only one thing that makes a dream impossible to achieve: the fear of failure."

"Tell your heart that the fear of suffering is worse than the suffering itself. And that no heart has ever suffered when it goes in search of its dreams, because every second of the search is a second's encounter with God and with eternity."

"Don't give in to your fears. If you do, you won't be able to talk to your heart."
- **Paulo Coelho** (*The Alchemist*)

"I must not fear. Fear is the mind-killer. Fear is the little-death that brings total obliteration. I will face my fear. I will permit it to pass over me and through me. And when it has gone past, I will turn the inner eye to see its path. Where the fear has gone there will be nothing. Only I will remain."
- **Frank Herbert** (*Dune*)

"Have no fear of perfection - you'll never reach it."
- **Salvador Dali**

"There are two basic motivating forces: fear and love. When we are afraid, we pull back from life. When we are in love, we open to all that life has to offer with passion, excitement, and acceptance. We need to learn to love ourselves first, in all our glory and our imperfections. If we cannot love ourselves, we cannot fully open to our ability to love others or our potential to create. Evolution and all hopes for a better world rest in the fearlessness and open-hearted vision of people who embrace life."
- **John Lennon**

"Men go to far greater lengths to avoid what they fear than to obtain what they desire."
- **Dan Brown** (*The DaVinci Code*)

"Don't be afraid of your fears. They're not there to scare you. They're there to let you know that something is worth it."
- **C. JoyBell C.**

"Nothing in life is to be feared, it is only to be understood. Now is the time to understand more, so that we may fear less."
- **Marie Curie**

"I have accepted fear as part of life – specifically the fear of change... I have gone ahead despite the pounding in the heart that says: turn back...."
- **Erica Jong**

"The only thing we have to fear is fear itself."
- **Franklin D. Roosevelt**

"He who has overcome his fears will truly be free."
- **Aristotle**

"What you fear most of all is —fear. Very wise..."
- **J.K. Rowling** (*Harry Potter and the Prisoner of Azkaban*)

"If you want to grow and be free to explore life, you cannot spend your life avoiding the myriad things that might hurt your heart or mind."

- **Singer, Michael A**. *The Untethered Soul: the journey beyond yourself,* New Harbinger / Noetic Books, 2007

"The key to growth is acknowledging your fear of the unknown and jumping in anyway."

- **Jen Sincero**

"Of all the liars in the world, sometimes the worst are our own fears."

- **Rudyard Kipling**

"Fear is only as deep as the mind allows."

- **Japanese Proverb**

"Courage is not the absence of fear, but rather the judgment that something else is more important than fear."

- **Ambrose Redmoon**

"The greatest mistake you can make in life is to be continually fearing you will make one."

- **E Hubbard**

"A mind focused on doubt and fear cannot focus on the journey to victory."

- **Mike Jones**

"When you feel pain, simply view it as energy. Just start seeing these inner experiences as energy passing through your heart and before the eye of your consciousness. Then relax. Do the opposite of contracting and closing. Relax and release. Relax your heart until you are actually face-to-face with the exact place where it hurts. Stay open and receptive so you can be present right where the tension is. ... This is very deep growth and transformation. But you will not want to do this. You will feel tremendous resistance to doing this, and that's what makes it so powerful. As you relax and feel the resistance, the heart will want to pull away, to close, to protect, and to defend itself. Keep relaxing. Relax your shoulders and relax your heart. Let go and give room for the pain to pass through you. It's just energy. Just see it as energy and let it go."

- **Singer, Michael A**. *The Untethered Soul: the journey beyond yourself,* New Harbinger / Noetic Books, 2007

Personal testimonial that this practice works. The challenge is, of course, to 'practice' relaxing and releasing *continuously*, since our mind, that voice in our head, is continuously inventing things to worry about (fear).

TIME

"The thing about time is that time isn't really real."
-   **James Taylor**

"Time isn't precious at all, because it is an illusion. What you perceive as precious is not time but the one point that is out of time: the Now. That is precious indeed. The more you are focused on time—past and future—the more you miss the Now, the most precious thing there is."
-   **Eckhart Tolle** (*The Power of Now: A Guide to Spiritual Enlightenment*)

"It's being here now that's important. There's no past and there's no future. Time is a very misleading thing. All there is ever, is the now. We can gain experience from the past, but we can't relive it; and we can hope for the future, but we don't know if there is one."
-   **George Harrison**

"Five minutes are enough to dream a whole life, that is how relative time is."
-   **Mario Benedetti**

"We are living in a culture entirely hypnotized by the illusion of time, in which the so-called present moment is felt as nothing but an infinitesimal hairline between an all-powerfully causative past and an absorbingly important future. We have no present. Our consciousness is almost completely preoccupied with memory and expectation. We

do not realize that there never was, is, nor will be any other experience than present experience. We are therefore out of touch with reality. We confuse the world as talked about, described, and measured with the world which actually is."
-   **Alan Wilson Watts**

"It's worth making time to find the things that really stir your soul. That's what makes you really feel alive. You have to say 'no' to other things you're used to, and do it with all your heart."
-   **Roy T. Bennett**

"The timeless in you is aware of life's timelessness. And knows that yesterday is but today's memory and tomorrow is today's dream."
-   **Khalil Gibran** (*The Prophet*)

"Lost Time is never found again."
-   **Benjamin Franklin** (*Poor Richard's Almanack*)

"When was the last time you spent a quiet moment just doing nothing – just sitting and looking at the sea, or watching the wind blowing the tree limbs, or waves rippling on a pond, a flickering candle or children playing in the park?"
-   **Ralph Marston**

"There comes a time when the world gets quiet and the only thing left is your own heart. So you'd better learn the sound of it. Otherwise you'll never understand what it's saying."
-   **Sarah Dessen** (*Just Listen*)

"It has been said, 'time heals all wounds.' I do not agree. The wounds remain. In time, the mind, protecting its sanity, covers them with scar tissue and the pain lessens. But it is never gone."
- **Rose Fitzgerald Kennedy**

"Don't waste your time in anger, regrets, worries, and grudges. Life is too short to be unhappy."
- **Roy T. Bennett**

"How did it get so late so soon?"
- **Dr. Seuss**

"Time is the longest distance between two places."
- **Tennessee Williams** (*The Glass Menagerie*)

"Time doesn't heal emotional pain; you need to learn how to let go."
- **Roy T. Bennett** (*The Light in the Heart*)

"Those who make the worst use of their time are the first to complain of its brevity."
- **Jean de La Bruyère** (*Les Caractères*)

"There's never enough time to do all the nothing you want."
- **Bill Watterson**

"Life is short. Focus on what really matters most. You have to change your priorities over time."
- **Roy T. Bennett** (*The Light in the Heart*)

"Sometimes I feel like if you just watch things, just sit still and let the world exist in front of you - sometimes I swear that just for a second time freezes and the world pauses in its tilt. Just for a second. And if you somehow found a way to live in that second, then you would live forever."

- **Lauren Oliver** (*Pandemonium*)

"Rest is not idleness, and to lie sometimes on the grass under trees on a summer's day, listening to the murmur of the water, or watching the clouds float across the sky, is by no means a waste of time."

- **John Lubbock** (*The Use Of Life*)

"Time is what we want most, but what we use worst."

- **William Penn**

MEDITATION
(FOR LAYMEN)

"The inner breakthrough to complete freedom is traditionally depicted by the overused and generally misunderstood term: 'enlightenment'. The problem is that our views of enlightenment are either based upon our personal experiences or upon our limited conceptual understanding. Since most people have never had experiences in this realm, the state of enlightenment is either scoffed at completely or viewed as the ultimate mystical state accessible to almost no one. It's safe to say that the only thing most people know for sure about enlightenment is that they are not there."

- **Singer, Michael A**. *The Untethered Soul: the journey beyond yourself*, New Harbinger / Noetic Books, 2007

"I have lived with several Zen masters -- all of them cats."

- **Eckhart Tolle** (*The Power of Now: A Guide to Spiritual Enlightenment*)

"If you want to conquer the anxiety of life, live in the moment, live in the breath."

- **Amit Ray** (*Om Chanting and Meditation*)

"Yoga is not a religion. It is a science, science of well-being, science of youthfulness, science of integrating body, mind and soul."

- **Amit Ray** (*Yoga and Vipassana: An Integrated Life Style*)

"Meditation is a journey to know yourself. Knowing yourself has many layers. Start knowing your bodily discomforts. Know your success, know your failures. Know your fears. Know your irritations. Know your pleasures, joy and happiness. Know your mental wounds. Go deeper and examine every feeling you have."

"It does not matter how long you are spending on the earth, how much money you have gathered or how much attention you have received. It is the amount of positive vibration you have radiated in life that matters,"

"Meditation is a way for nourishing and blossoming the divinity within you."

"Looking at beauty in the world, is the first step of purifying the mind."

- **Amit Ray** (*Meditation: Insights and Inspirations*)

"I'm simply saying that there is a way to be sane. I'm saying that you can get rid of all this insanity created by the past in you. Just by being a simple witness of your thought processes. It is simply sitting silently, witnessing the thoughts, passing before you. Just witnessing, not interfering not even judging, because the moment you judge you have lost the pure witness. The moment you say "this is good, this is bad," you have already jumped onto the thought process.

It takes a little time to create a gap between the witness and the mind. Once the gap is there, you are in for a great surprise, that you are not the mind, that you are the witness, a watcher.

And this process of watching is the very alchemy of real religion. Because as you become more and more deeply rooted in witnessing, thoughts start disappearing. You are, but the mind is utterly empty.

That's the moment of enlightenment. That is the moment that you become…a really free human being."
- **Osho**

"To understand the immeasurable, the mind must be extraordinarily quiet, still."
- **Jiddu Krishnamurti**

"Sometimes you need to sit lonely on the floor in a quiet room in order to hear your own voice and not let it drown in the noise of others."
- **Charlotte Eriksson** (*You're Doing Just Fine*)

"If you just sit and observe, you will see how restless your mind is. If you try to calm it, it only makes it worse, but over time it does calm, and when it does, there's room to hear more subtle things - that's when your intuition starts to blossom and you start to see things more clearly and be in the present more. Your mind just slows down, and you see a tremendous expanse in the moment. You see so much more than you could see before. It's a discipline; you have to practice it."

- **Walter Isaacson** (*Steve Jobs*)

"Your consciousness knows no death, no birth- It is only your body that is born and dies- But you are not aware of your consciousness- You are not conscious of your consciousness- And that is the whole art of meditation; Becoming conscious of consciousness itself."

- **Osho**

"The easiest way to get in touch with this universal power is through silent Prayer. Shut your eyes, shut your mouth, and open your heart. This is the golden rule of prayer. Prayer should be soundless words coming forth from the centre of your heart filled with love."

- **Amit Ray** (*Om Chanting and Meditation*)

"Meditation is an essential travel partner on your journey of personal transformation. Meditation connects you with your soul, and this connection gives you access to your intuition, your heartfelt desires, your integrity, and the inspiration to create a life you love."

- **Sarah McLean**

"I believe that reading and writing are the most nourishing forms of meditation anyone has so far found. By reading the writings of the most interesting minds in history, we meditate with our own minds and theirs as well. This to me is a miracle."

- **Kurt Vonnegut** (*Palm Sunday: An Autobiographical Collage*)

Rather than paraphrasing, I quoted Mr. Vonnegut verbatim because (literally) I couldn't have said it better myself.

This is the purpose of this book in a nutshell, specifically, sharing my meditations on the writings of the "most interesting mind" of Mr. Michael A. Singer.

The reason for this chapter's title: *Meditation (for laymen)* is that I have no intention of trying to explain (or even beginning to understand myself) all of the definitions, nuances, beliefs and practices of: The Stages of Enlightenment, Yoga, Zen, Buddhism, Hinduism, G-d, Inner Being, Mantras, Atma, Satori, Mahamudra, Nirvana, Tao, The Kingdom of God, etc.

For me, just learning how to place one foot on the path to the "journey beyond yourself" would be a major accomplishment.

MUSIC

In my opinion, one cannot discuss the Soul, Spirituality, etc. without including the subject of music. I never truly appreciated music until Nancy. Of all the gifts she gave to me, the love of music may have been the greatest.

"Nancy was the embodiment of music, and Music was the 'soul' of Nancy Bohart. And, because of Nancy, music is now my link to her *Untethered Soul*".
- **David F. Combs** (*Nancy & Dave ... A Love Story*)

"Without Music, Life Would be a Mistake."
- **Friedrich Nietzche**

"Music expresses that which cannot be put into words and that which cannot remain silent"
- **Victor Hugo**

"After silence, that which comes nearest to expressing the inexpressible is music."
- **Aldous Huxley** (*Music at Night and Other Essays*)

"If I should ever die, God forbid, let this be my epitaph: THE ONLY PROOF HE NEEDED FOR THE EXISTENCE OF GOD WAS MUSIC"
- **Kurt Vonnegut**

"Life, he realized, was much like a song. In the beginning there is mystery, in the end there is confirmation, but it's in

the middle where all the emotion resides to make the whole thing worthwhile."
-   **Nicholas Sparks** (*The Last Song*)

"Ah, music," he said, wiping his eyes. "A magic beyond all we do here!"
-   **J.K. Rowling** (*Harry Potter and the Sorcerer's Stone*)

"Where words leave off, music begins."
-   **Heinrich Heine**

"There are two means of refuge from the misery of life — music and cats."
-   **Albert Schweitzer**

"The only truth is music."
-   **Jack Kerouac**

"Music is...A higher revelation than all Wisdom & Philosophy"
-   **Ludwig van Beethoven**

"Music is to the soul what words are to the mind."
-   **Modest Mouse** (*Modest Mouse – Good News for People Who Love Bad News*)

"Music, once admitted to the soul, becomes a sort of spirit, and never dies."
-   **Edward Bulwer Lytton**

"Music is the universal language of mankind."
-   **Henry Wadsworth Longfellow**

"To stop the flow of music would be like the stopping of time itself, incredible and inconceivable."
- **Aaron Copland**

"Music . . . can name the unnameable and communicate the unknowable."
- **Leonard Bernstein**

"A painter paints pictures on canvas. But musicians paint their pictures on silence."
- **Leopold Stokowski**

"The music is not in the notes, but in the silence between."
- **Wolfgang Amadeus Mozart**

"Music in the soul can be heard by the universe."
- **Lao Tzu**

"Music is the language of the spirit. It opens the secret of life bringing peace, abolishing strife."
- **Kahlil Gibran**

"Music... will help dissolve your perplexities and purify your character and sensibilities, and in time of care and sorrow, will keep a fountain of joy alive in you."
- **Dietrich Bonhoeffer**

"I love the relationship that anyone has with music ... because there's something in us that is beyond the reach of words, something that eludes and defies our best attempts to spit it out. ... It's the best part of us probably ..."
- **Nick Hornby** (*Songbook*)

"Music acts like a magic key, to which the most tightly closed heart opens."
- **Maria von Trapp**

"Music produces a kind of pleasure which human nature cannot do without."
- **Confucius** (*The Book of Rites*)

"Music is my higher power"
- **Oliver James**

"Music is an outburst of the soul."
- **Frederick Delius**

"Life seems to go on without effort when I am filled with music."
- **George Eliot** (*The Mill on the Floss*)

"If it weren't for music, I would think that love is mortal."
- **Mark Helprin** (*A Soldier of the Great War*)

"People ask me how I make music. I tell them I just step into it. It's like stepping into a river and joining the flow. Every moment in the river has its song."
- **Michael Jackson**

"If music be the food of love, play on."
- **William Shakespeare** (*Twelfth Night*)

"Joy, sorrow, tears, lamentation, laughter -- to all these music gives voice, but in such a way that we are transported from the world of unrest to a world of peace, and see reality

in a new way, as if we were sitting by a mountain lake and contemplating hills and woods and clouds in the tranquil and fathomless water."
-   **Albert Schweitzer**

"If Music is a Place -- then Jazz is the City, Folk is the Wilderness, Rock is the Road, Classical is a Temple."
-   **Vera Nazarian**

"We are the ones who take this thing called music and line it up with this thing called time. We are the ticking, we are the pulsing, we are underneath every part of this moment. And by making the moment our own, we are rendering it timeless."
-   **Rachel Cohn** (*Nick & Norah's Infinite Playlist*)

"All the good music has already been written by people with wigs and stuff."
-   **Frank Zappa**

"When I am ..... completely myself, entirely alone... or during the night when I cannot sleep, it is on such occasions that my ideas flow best and most abundantly. Whence and how these ideas come I know not nor can I force them."
-   **Wolfgang Amadeus Mozart**

"Music is the divine way to tell beautiful, poetic things to the heart."
-   **Pablo Casals**

"Bach is an astronomer, discovering the most marvelous stars. Beethoven challenges the universe. I only try to express the soul and the heart of man."
- **Frédéric Chopin**

"Music isn't just a pleasure, a transient satisfaction. It's a need, a deep hunger; and when the music is right, it's joy. Love. A foretaste of heaven. A comfort in grief. Is it too much to think that perhaps God speaks to us sometimes through music? How, then, could I be so ungrateful as to refuse the message?"
- **Orson Scott Card**

"Music brings a warm glow to my vision, thawing mind and muscle from their endless wintering."
- **Haruki Murakami** (*Hard-Boiled Wonderland and the End of the World*)

"Words make you think. Music makes you feel. A song makes you feel a thought."
- **Yip Harburg**

"Music, when soft voices die, vibrates in the memory."
- **Percy Bysshe Shelley** (The Complete Poems)

"No matter who we are, no matter what our circumstances, our feelings and emotions are universal. And music has always been a great way to make people aware of that connection. It can help you open up a part of yourself and express feelings you didn't know you were feeling. It's risky to let that happen. But it's a risk you have to take-because only then will you find you're not alone."

-   **Josh Groban**

"Music is the one incorporeal entrance into the higher world of knowledge which comprehends mankind but which mankind cannot comprehend."

-   **Ludwig van Beethoven**

"I'm wishing he could see that music lives. Forever. That it's stronger than death. Stronger than time. And that its strength holds you together when nothing else can."

-   **Jennifer Donnelly** (*Revolution*)

"Music gives color to the air of the moment."

-   **Karl Lagerfeld**

NATURE

I used to occasionally marvel at Mother Nature, like we all have – occasionally, e.g. a beautiful sunset, the ocean, a Redwood forest, etc., but since widowed, retired and on my own (for the first time in my life), I find myself *frequently* noticing nature … even before discovering *The Untethered Soul*, where Mr. Singer makes numerous references to observing nature, especially when seeking to find one's Self, that 'Seat of Consciousness', from where one can observe the inner voice, the inner turmoil/pain, the psyche, the blockages of the heart, etc. in the same objective way as one observes external stimuli.

"There is a pleasure in the pathless woods,
There is a rapture on the lonely shore,
There is society, where none intrudes,
By the deep sea, and music in its roar:
I love not man the less, but Nature more"
   -   **Lord Byron**

"The clearest way into the Universe is through a forest wilderness."
"The mountains are calling and I must go."
   -   **John Muir**

"I like this place and could willingly waste my time in it."
   -   **William Shakespeare**

"The best remedy for those who are afraid, lonely or unhappy is to go outside, somewhere where they can be quite alone with the heavens, nature and God. Because only then does one feel that all is as it should be and that God wishes to see people happy, amidst the simple beauty of nature. As longs as this exists, and it certainly always will, I know that then there will always be comfort for every sorrow, whatever the circumstances may be. And I firmly believe that nature brings solace in all troubles."
- **Anne Frank** (*The Diary of a Young Girl*)

"Adopt the pace of nature: her secret is patience."
- **Ralph Waldo Emerson**

"Those who contemplate the beauty of the earth find reserves of strength that will endure as long as life lasts. There is something infinitely healing in the repeated refrains of nature -- the assurance that dawn comes after night, and spring after winter."
- **Rachel Carson** (*Silent Spring*)

"We need the tonic of wildness...At the same time that we are earnest to explore and learn all things, we require that all things be mysterious and unexplorable, that land and sea be indefinitely wild, unsurveyed and unfathomed by us because unfathomable. We can never have enough of nature."
- **Henry David Thoreau** (*Walden: Or, Life in the Woods*)

"Nature is not a place to visit. It is home."
- **Gary Snyder**

"Looking at beauty in the world, is the first step of purifying the mind."
- **Amit Ray** (*Meditation: Insights and Inspirations*)

"Rest is not idleness, and to lie sometimes on the grass under trees on a summer's day, listening to the murmur of the water, or watching the clouds float across the sky, is by no means a waste of time."
- **John Lubbock** (*The Use Of Life*)

"I believe in God, only I spell it Nature."
- **Frank Lloyd Wright** (*Truth Against the World: Frank Lloyd Wright Speaks for an Organic Architecture*)

"Imitate the trees. Learn to lose in order to recover, and remember that nothing stays the same for long, not even pain, psychic pain. Sit it out. Let it all pass. Let it go."
- **May Sarton** (*Journal of a Solitude*)

"Landscapes of great wonder and beauty lie under our feet and all around us. They are discovered in tunnels in the ground, the heart of flowers, the hollows of trees, fresh-water ponds, seaweed jungles between tides, and even drops of water. Life in these hidden worlds is more startling in reality than anything we can imagine. How could this earth of ours, which is only a speck in the heavens, have so much variety of life, so many curious and exciting creatures?"
- **Walt Disney**

"The lover of nature is he whose inward and outward senses are still truly adjusted to each other; who has retained the spirit of infancy even into the era of manhood. His intercourse with heaven and earth, becomes part of his daily food. In the presence of nature, a wild delight runs through the man, in spite of real sorrows..."

- **Ralph Waldo Emerson** (*Nature and Walking*)

"I still find each day too short for all the thoughts I want to think, all the walks I want to take, all the books I want to read, and all the friends I want to see. The longer I live, the more my mind dwells upon the beauty and the wonder of the world."

- **John Burroughs**

SPIRITUALITY

"Make your own Bible. Select and collect all the words and sentences that in all your readings have been to you like the blast of a trumpet."
-   **Ralph Waldo Emerson**

This is exactly what I am trying to do with this book ...

"Spirituality is the commitment to go beyond, no matter what it takes. It's an infinite journey based upon going beyond yourself every minute of every day for the rest of your life. If you're truly going beyond, you are always at your limits. You're never back in the comfort zone. A spiritual being feels as though they are always against that edge, and they are constantly being pushed through it."

"The spiritual journey is one of constant transformation. In order to grow, you must give up the struggle to remain the same, and learn to embrace change at all times."
-   **Singer, Michael A**. *The Untethered Soul: the journey beyond yourself*, New Harbinger / Noetic Books, 2007

"I believe in God, but not as one thing, not as an old man in the sky. I believe that what people call God is something in all of us. I believe that what Jesus and Mohammed and Buddha and all the rest said was right. It's just that the translations have gone wrong."
-   **John Lennon**

"The possession of knowledge does not kill the sense of wonder and mystery. There is always more mystery."
- **Anais Nin**

"We are not human beings having a spiritual experience. We are spiritual beings having a human experience."
- **Pierre Teilhard de Chardin**

"Science is not only compatible with spirituality; it is a profound source of spirituality. When we recognize our place in an immensity of light-years and in the passage of ages, when we grasp the intricacy, beauty, and subtlety of life, then that soaring feeling, that sense of elation and humility combined, is surely spiritual. So are our emotions in the presence of great art or music or literature, or acts of exemplary selfless courage such as those of Mohandas Gandhi or Martin Luther King, Jr. The notion that science and spirituality are somehow mutually exclusive does a disservice to both."
- **Carl Sagan** (*The Demon-Haunted World: Science as a Candle in the Dark*)

"I don't understand why people insist on pitting concepts of evolution and creation against each other. Why can't they see that spiritualism and science are one? That bodies evolve and souls evolve and the universe is a fluid package that marries them both in a wonderful package called a human being. What's wrong with that idea?"
- **Garth Stein** (*The Art of Racing in the Rain*)

"I'm not afraid of death because I don't believe in it. It's just getting out of one car, and into another."
- **John Lennon**

"A quiet conscience makes one strong!"
- **Anne Frank** (*The Diary of a Young Girl*)

"When you connect to the silence within you, that is when you can make sense of the disturbance going on around you."
- **Stephen Richards**

"Love goes very far beyond the physical person of the beloved. It finds its deepest meaning in his spiritual being, his inner self. Whether or not he is actually present, whether or not he is still alive at all, ceases somehow to be of importance."
- **Viktor E. Frankl** (*Man's Search for Meaning*)

"The resting place of the mind is the heart. The only thing the mind hears all day is clanging bells and noise and argument, and all it wants is quietude. The only place the mind will ever find peace is inside the silence of the heart. That's where you need to go."
- **Elizabeth Gilbert** (*Eat, Pray, Love*)

"Crying is one of the highest devotional songs. One who knows crying, knows spiritual practice. If you can cry with a pure heart, nothing else compares to such a prayer. Crying includes all the principles of Yoga."
- **Kripalvanandji**

"You were born a child of light's wonderful secret— you return to the beauty you have always been."
- **Aberjhani** (*Visions of a Skylark Dressed in Black*)

"The spiritual life does not remove us from the world but leads us deeper into it"
- **Nouwen Henri J. M.**

"Self-talk reflects your innermost feelings."
- **Dr. Asa Don Brown**

"An awake heart is like a sky that pours light."
- **Hafiz**

"As soon as you look at the world through an ideology you are finished. No reality fits an ideology. Life is beyond that. … That is why people are always searching for a meaning to life… Meaning is only found when you go beyond meaning. Life only makes sense when you perceive it as mystery and it makes no sense to the conceptualizing mind."
- **Anthony de Mello**

"Spirituality is recognizing and celebrating that we are all inextricably connected to each other by a power greater than all of us, and that our connection to that power and to one another is grounded in love and compassion. Practicing spirituality brings a sense of perspective, meaning and purpose to our lives."
- **Brené Brown** (*The Gifts of Imperfection*)

"Soul connections are not often found and are worth every bit of fight left in you to keep."
- **Shannon Alder**

"The first peace, which is the most important, is that which comes within the souls of people when they realize

their relationship, their oneness with the universe and all its powers, and when they realize at the center of the universe dwells the Great Spirit, and that its center is really everywhere, it is within each of us."
- **Black Elk**

"Anyone who is steady in his determination for the advanced stage of spiritual realization and can equally tolerate the onslaughts of distress and happiness is certainly a person eligible for liberation."
- **A.C. Bhaktivedanta Swami Prabhupada** (*The Bhagavad-gita*)

"Your life is your spiritual path. It's what's right in front of you. You can't live anyone else's life. The task is to live yours and stop trying to copy one you think looks better."
- **Sandy Nathan** (*Stepping Off the Edge: Learning & Living Spiritual Practices*)

"Nothing in all creation is so like God as stillness."
- **Meister Eckhart**

"The sea is only the embodiment of a supernatural and wonderful existence. It is nothing but love and emotion; it is the 'Living Infinite...'"
- **Jules Verne**

"Perhaps our dreams are there to be broken, and our plans are there to crumble, and our tomorrows are there to dissolve into todays, and perhaps all of this is all a giant invitation to wake up from the dream of separation, to awaken from the mirage of control, and embrace whole-heartedly what ιs present. Perhaps it is all a call to compassion, to a deep embrace of this universe in all its bliss and pain and bittersweet glory. Perhaps we were never really in control of our lives, and perhaps we are constantly invited to remember this, since we constantly forget it. Perhaps suffering is not the enemy at all, and at its core, there is a first-hand, real-time lesson we must all learn, if we are to be truly human, and truly divine. Perhaps breakdown always contains breakthrough. Perhaps suffering is simply a rite of passage, not a test or a punishment, nor a signpost to something in the future or past, but a direct pointer to the mystery of existence itself, here and now. Perhaps life cannot go 'wrong' at all."

- **Jeff Foster**

"When we let go of our battles and open our heart to things as they are, then we come to rest in the present moment. This is the beginning and the end of spiritual practice. Only in this moment can we discover that which is timeless. Only here can we find the love that we seek. Love in the past is simply memory, and love in the future is fantasy. Only in the reality of the present can we love, can we awaken, can we find peace and understanding and connection with ourselves and the world."

- **Jack Kornfield** (*A Path with Heart: A Guide Through the Perils and Promises of Spiritual Life*)

"We're all pieces of the same ever-changing puzzle; some connected for mere seconds, some connected for life, some connected through knowledge, some through belief, some connected through wisdom, some through Love, and some connected with no explanation at all. Yet, as spiritual being having a human experience, we're all here for the sensations this reality or illusion has to offer. The best anyone can hope for is the right to be able to Live, Learn, Love then Leave. After that, reap the benefits of their own chosen existence in the hereafter by virtue of simply believing in what they believe. As for here, it took me a while but this progression helped me with my life: "I like myself. I Love myself. I am myself."

- **Stanley Victor Paskavich**

"There is far more spiritual potential within than most people realize. The potential is so great that to define it in words would be impossible."

- **Belsebuub** (*Gazing into the Eternal: Reflections upon a Deeper Purpose to Living*)

"Spirituality is not adopting more beliefs and assumptions but uncovering the best in you."

- **Amit Ray** (*Beautify your Breath – Beautify your Life*)

"As spiritual searchers we need to become freer and freer of the attachment to our own smallness in which we get occupied with me-me-me. Pondering on large ideas or standing in front of things which remind us of a vast scale can free us from acquisitiveness and competitiveness and from our likes and dislikes. If we sit with an increasing stillness of the body, and attune our mind to the sky or to the ocean or to the myriad stars at night, or any other indicators of vastness, the mind gradually stills and the heart is filled with quiet joy. Also recalling our own experiences in which we acted generously or with compassion for the simple delight of it without expectation of any gain can give us more confidence in the existence of a deeper goodness from which we may deviate. (39)"

- **Ravi Ravindra** (*The Wisdom of Patenjali's Yoga Sutras: A New Translation and Guide by Ravi Ravindra*)

"You are not limited to this body, to this mind, or to this reality—you are a limitless ocean of Consciousness, imbued with infinite potential. You are existence itself."

- **Joseph P. Kauffman** (*The Answer is YOU: A Guide to Mental, Emotional, and Spiritual Freedom*)

"And once you've been to this Center, this Truth, you'll know your way everywhere. You are never lost again."

- **David Housholder** (*The Blackberry Bush*)

"Thoughts don't become things; thoughts ARE things."

- **Eric Micha'el Leventhal**

"Enlightenment is: absolute cooperation with the inevitable."

- **Anthony de Mello**

"...What you are is a force--a force that makes it possible for your body to live, a force that makes it possible for your whole mind to dream...You are life"

- **Miguel Ruiz** (*The Mastery of Love: A Practical Guide to the Art of Relationship – Toltec Wisdom Book*)

"May the Force be With You."

- **Yoda**

PERSPECTIVE, KINDNESS & OTHER RANDOM THOUGHTS

"You wouldn't worry so much about what others think of you if you realized how seldom they do."
-   **Eleanor Roosevelt**

"What people in the world think of you is really none of your business."
-   **Martha Graham**

"The Paradoxical Commandments
People are illogical, unreasonable, and self-centered. Love them anyway.

If you do good, people will accuse you of selfish ulterior motives. Do good anyway.

If you are successful, you will win false friends and true enemies. Succeed anyway.

The good you do today will be forgotten tomorrow. Do good anyway.

Honesty and frankness make you vulnerable. Be honest and frank anyway.

The biggest men and women with the biggest ideas can be shot down by the smallest men and women with the smallest minds. Think big anyway.

People favor underdogs but follow only top dogs. Fight for a few underdogs anyway

What you spend years building may be destroyed overnight. Build anyway.
People really need help but may attack you if you do help them. Help people anyway.
Give the world the best you have and you'll get kicked in the teeth. Give the world the best you have anyway."
- **Kent M. Keith** (*The Silent Revolution: Dynamic Leadership in the Student Council*)

"Indifference and neglect often do much more damage than outright dislike."
- **J.K. Rowling** (*Harry Potter and the Order of the Phoenix*)

A few quotes taken from some Facebook posts …

"When you understand that what most people really, really want is simply to feel good about themselves, and when you realize that with just a few well-chosen words you can help virtually anyone on the planet instantly achieve this, you begin to realize just how simple life is, how powerful you are, and that love is the key."
- **Mike Dooley**

"You never really know the true impact you have on those around you. You never know how much someone needed that smile you gave them. You never know how much your kindness turned someone's entire life around. You never know how much someone needed that long hug or deep talk. So don't wait for someone else to be kind first. Don't wait for better circumstances or for someone to change.

Just be kind, because you never know how much someone needs it."

-   **Unknown**

"Sometimes you have to let go of the picture of what you thought life would be like and learn to find joy in the story you're living."

-   **Unknown**

"… We leave you a tradition with a future. The tender loving care of human beings will never become obsolete.

People even more than things have to be restored, renewed, revived, reclaimed and redeemed and redeemed and redeemed. Never throw out anybody.

Remember, if you ever need a helping hand, you'll find one at the end of your arm.

As you grow older, you will discover that you have two hands: one for helping yourself, the other for helping others. Your 'good old days' are still ahead of you, may you have many of them."

-   **Sam Levenson** (*In One Era & Out the Other*)

"Be kind, for everyone you meet is fighting a harder battle."

-   **Plato**

"Attitude is a choice. Happiness is a choice. Optimism is a choice. Kindness is a choice. Giving is a choice. Respect is a choice. Whatever choice you make makes you. Choose wisely."

-   **Roy T. Bennett** (*The Light in the Heart*)

"Do your little bit of good where you are; it's those little bits of good put together that overwhelm the world."
- **Desmond Tutu**

"Guard well within yourself that treasure, kindness. Know how to give without hesitation, how to lose without regret, how to acquire without meanness."
- **George Sand**

"How would your life be different if…You stopped making negative judgmental assumptions about people you encounter? Let today be the day…You look for the good in everyone you meet and respect their journey."
- **Steve Maraboli** (*Life, the Truth, and Being Free*)

"Tenderness and kindness are not signs of weakness and despair, but manifestations of strength and resolution."
- **Kahlil Gibran**

"Kindness in words creates confidence. Kindness in thinking creates profoundness. Kindness in giving creates love."
- **Lao-Tzu**

"The fact that we live at the bottom of a deep gravity well, on the surface of a gas covered planet going around a nuclear fireball 90 million miles away and think this to be normal is obviously some indication of how skewed our perspective tends to be."
- **Douglas Adams** (*The Salmon of Doubt: Hitchhiking the Galaxy One Last Time*)

"There are no facts, only interpretations."
- **Friedrich Nietzsche**

"Some people see the glass half full. Others see it half empty. I see a glass that's twice as big as it needs to be."
- **George Carlin**

"Most misunderstandings in the world could be avoided if people would simply take the time to ask, "What else could this mean?"
- **Shannon L. Alder**

"The cosmos is within us. We are made of star-stuff. We are a way for the universe to know itself."
- **Carl Sagan**

"In all affairs it's a healthy thing now and then to hang a question mark on the things you have long taken for granted."
- **Bertrand Russell**

"It is a narrow mind which cannot look at a subject from various points of view."
- **George Eliot** (*Middlemarch*)

"There is a huge amount of freedom that comes to you when you take nothing personally."
- **Don Miguel Ruiz** (*The Four Agreements: A Practical Guide to Personal Freedom*)

"If someone does not want me it is not the end of the world. But if I do not want me, the world is nothing but endings."
- **Nayyirah Waheed**

"The trick to forgetting the big picture is to look at everything close up."
- **Chuck Palahniuk**

"If we climb high enough, we will reach a height from which tragedy ceases to look tragic."
- **Irvin D. Yalom** (*When Nietzche Wept*)

"If we are always arriving and departing, it is also true that we are eternally anchored. One's destination is never a place but rather a new way of looking at things."
- **Henry Miller** (*Big Sur and the Oranges of Hieronymus Bosch*)

"The distance between insanity and genius is measured only by success"
- **Ian Fleming**

"If the stars should appear but one night every thousand years how man would marvel and adore."
- **Ralph Waldo Emerson**

"It suddenly struck me that that tiny pea, pretty and blue, was the Earth. I put up my thumb and shut one eye, and my thumb blotted out the planet Earth. I didn't feel like a giant. I felt very, very small."
- **Neil Armstrong**

"Distance lends enchantment to the view."
- **Mark Twain**

"All people at root are time optimists. We always think there's enough time to do things with other people. Time to say things to them. And then something happens and then we stand there holding on to words like 'if'."
- **Fredrik Backman** (*A Man Called Ove*)

"The best things in life aren't things."
- **Art Buchwald**

On a personal 'random thoughts' note: I now realize that I spent my whole life looking for (and worrying about) the approval of others, e.g. parents, teachers, coaches, friends, girlfriends, Nancy, bosses, society, strangers, etc. I believe that 'with age comes wisdom', and doubly so when you are widowed and retired from your career. Being on your own, without a spouse, children, a career, etc. gives one the opportunity for deeper thoughts/insight beyond the daily routine most of us get accustomed to. Time to think. Time for some introspection. Time for potential growth opportunities.

Travel is a good thing, in my opinion, as it gives you the chance to explore things you have never seen, experience nature, visit with family and friends, make new connections, and expand your mind. During my working life, I traveled a lot by car (primarily Southern California), but it wasn't until my 'second life' these last few years that I traveled for pleasure, having made several cross-country road trips by car and train, and even an impromptu car trip up to the

Canadian Rockies. I always enjoyed driving because it was the perfect time to think, to relax, to listen to music, and to be on your own. After reading Mr. Singer's *The Untethered Soul*, I now realize it would also be the perfect opportunity to practice some of his Self-awareness techniques (and will be doing so during future road trips, I assure you.)

Also, for me, writing is a good thing, allowing for the exploration of 'revisited' thoughts and feelings, documenting the past, and remembering life's events and people. This is what I did with my first two (self-published) books about my career and my life-long love, Nancy ... i.e. writing about what I know. **With this latest book of quotes, I am attempting to write about what I *want* to know.**

Compiling and reading the many quotes and book excerpts used in this book ... all from people wiser than I ... provided me with many insights and many opportunities for reflection (introspection.) I now realize that worrying about things, whether trivial or seemingly significant, is pointless, because 99% of those things either never happen and/or are completely out of our control. Being somewhat of a 'control freak' and stress-management expert my whole life, this comes as a true revelation. I always prided myself on controlling potential disasters, "putting out fires" and preparing for worst-case scenarios. Now I see how much energy was wasted on these life-long efforts.

I was taught that stress is simply our internal physical reaction to lack of control. A perfect example is job stress, because most of us have very little control over the demands of our jobs, our boss, our coworkers, our work environment, etc. What I have learned is that we DO (or can) have control over how we consciously process "stress factors". Although the manifestations of stress on our body are physical, the stress/worry itself is mental – it all starts (and hopefully stops) in the mind. If we can learn to step back and consciously "witness" what is going on in our mind, and then "relax and release" those negative influencers, we can be happy and stress-free. As I said early on, easier said than done, but just consider the benefits of this 'journey' versus the continuing journey you are currently on. Or, in other words, "How is that working for you?"

Or, in *other* words (paraphrased from *AA Serenity Prayer*) ... "God grant me the serenity to accept the things I cannot change; courage to change the things I can; and wisdom to know the difference."

I realize that young people, young professionals, and especially young parents have a LOT on their plate, and that introspection, reflection and the search for life's meaning are very low on the priority list. My only suggestion is that ... you are never too young to try to understand the mystery (secret) of life, and that time is relative. Sure, it is much easier for an older widower/retiree to find the time for self-reflection, introspection, and the search for understanding, BUT it is never too early to put a foot in the water to better understanding life's 'journey', and understanding how to better experience, i.e. manage, life's joys and sorrows.

We have all heard the phrase, "Youth is wasted on the young", and all this means to me is that, as we age and have life experiences, we realize that, if I knew *then* what

I know now, I might have made other choices. But such is the nature of life. Youth belongs to the young. We have all been there – for good or for bad. Experience – don't waste it. Learn from it. Never let the indiscretions or heartbreaks of youth keep you from loving and enjoying life. Just don't 'cling' to those old/past memories/heartaches. Let them go ("relax and release"). Learn to be happy, wherever you are in life's journey.

"Billions of things are going on in this world. You can think about it all you want, but life is still going to keep on happening."

- **Singer, Michael A**. *The Untethered Soul: the journey beyond yourself,* New Harbinger / Noetic Books, 2007

ENLIGHTENED A BIT

As I mentioned earlier, the process of compiling complementary quotes, excerpts and thoughts for this book was really an exercise to help me better understand the teachings of the "conscious use of the consciousness" in Michael Singer's *The Untethered Soul: the journey beyond yourself*. As any educator can tell you, the teacher always learns more about the subject matter than the students. This was my thinking here.

I originally bought the book to help me along the path of recovery following the greatest loss I have ever experienced, thinking that the book was about Life After Death ... only to discover that it is really about Life BEFORE Death (the *true* Secret of Life.) Although still very much a Freshman in my understanding, I have come to realize that most of us are unaware of our true Self, since our consciousness is 'tethered' to our self-image (ego), and that very few of us will ever achieve Enlightenment, that state of mind where true inner freedom and liberation can be realized.

I am by no means enlightened, but I do feel 'lighter', having lifted ("released") some of the pain from my heart.

In my opinion, Mr. Singer did an expert job of joining Eastern and Western religions & philosophies ... in laymen's terms, showing that they are all similar when it comes to **The Path of Unconditional Happiness** (Chapter 15: *Singer,*

Michael A. The Untethered Soul: the journey beyond yourself,
New Harbinger / Noetic Books, 2007) ...

"The highest spiritual path is life itself. If you know how to live daily life, it all becomes a liberating experience. ... you have to realize that you really only have one choice in this life, and it's not about your career, whom you want to marry, or whether you want to seek God. People tend to burden themselves with so many choices. But, in the end, you can throw it all away and just make one basic, underlying decision. Do you want to be happy, or do you not want to be happy? It's really that simple. Once you make that choice, your path through life becomes totally clear."

"... If you decide that you're going to be happy from now on for the rest of your life, you will not only be happy, you will become enlightened. Unconditional happiness is the highest technique there is. You don't have to learn Sanskrit or read any scriptures. You don't have to renounce the world. You just have to really mean it regardless of what happens. This is truly a spiritual path, and it is as direct and sure a path to Awakening as could possibly exist."

"The key to staying happy is really very simple ... If you look inside, you will see that when you're happy, your heart feels open and the energy rushes up inside of you. When you aren't happy, your heart feels closed and no energy comes up inside. So to stay happy, just don't close your heart. No matter what happens, even if your wife leaves you or your husband dies, you don't close."

"Unconditional happiness is a very high path and a very high technique because it solves everything. You could learn yoga techniques, such as meditation and postures, but what do you do with the rest of your life? The technique of unconditional happiness is ideal because what you're doing with the rest of your life is already defined – you're letting go of yourself so that you can remain happy."

Author's note: Although Mr. Singer does an excellent job in simplifying his message about Unconditional Happiness, the "how to" is still the real trick ... and for these tips/suggestions, you will need to read his book yourself. My intent with this *composition of quotes* book is simply to complement and support Mr. Singer's teachings, which I found most "enlightening", through the use of quotes/excerpts from other great minds, and to share my personal thoughts on a few subjects addressed in *The Untethered Soul: the journey beyond yourself.*

Perhaps, in the *simplest* of terms possible, try to live life this way:

Don't Worry Be Happy
-    **Bobby McFerrin**

REFERENCES

Singer, Michael A. *The Untethered Soul: the journey beyond yourself*, New Harbinger / Noetic Books, 2007

(Excerpts Republished with Permission of New Harbinger Publications, from The Untethered Soul: the journey beyond yourself, Michael A. Singer, 1 edition, October 3, 2007; permission conveyed through Copyright Clearance Center, Inc.)

GoodReads. Accessed July 2020, https://www.goodreads.com/quotes/tag

Printed in the United States
By Bookmasters